MY BOOK

Joy

by
Mary E. Boyd
Illustrated by
Joan Drescher

Stardust
Books

THE C. R. GIBSON COMPANY
Publishers
NORWALK, CONNECTICUT

Stardust
Books

Copyright © MCMLXIX by
The C. R. Gibson Company, Norwalk, Connecticut
All rights reserved
Printed in the United States of America
Library of Congress Catalog Card Number: 69-12372
S.B.N. 8378-1919-9

Joy can come as a frolicsome thing,
A boy at play, a kite on a string.

Joy's a kitten
  as soft as silk,
With a pink little tongue
  for lapping milk.

Joy can be when
you swell with pride
At the thrill of your
very first pony ride.

Or a wiggly fish on the end of a hook
Which you snatched right out of a chattery brook.

It's a trip with friends
for a picnic lunch;
It's gathering flowers
in a bunch.

Joy's a clown in a tall red hat,

Or maybe a swinging acrobat.

Joy's a search
    for the things you prize —
Tadpoles that wriggle
    and butterflies.

Joy can come
    when you climb a tree,
Or run barefoot
    on a country spree.

It's a swim for two in the summertime,

Or it may be finding a shiny dime.

It's a baseball game in the afternoon.

It's a lollipop and a red balloon.

Joy's a ride on a Ferris wheel,
Where no one minds if you laugh and squeal.

Joy can come too
    in a quiet way,
When you visit
    a sick little friend one day,

And you gladly share
    with your very best chum,
A piece of your favorite
    bubble gum.

It's a joy to sit
   with a friend and look
At all of the things
   in his picture book.

It's the warm contentment
you feel inside,
Such a happy feeling
it's hard to hide.

Joy's a hug
    and a kiss goodnight,
And a million things
    that are all just right.

It's the love you feel
    when you softly say,
"Thank you, God,"
    at the close of day.